Apples, cherries, Red Raspberries

to Sister Mary Jude, my first-grade teacher in Mission, Kansas
—B.P.C.

to my parents, as proof that the fruit did not fall far from the tree
—M.G.

Fruit:
The part of a plant that contains seeds. Fruits can usually be eaten. Most fruits taste sweet.

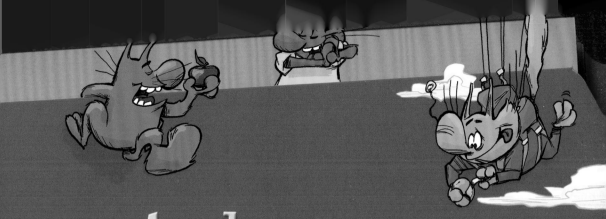

Apples, Cherries, Red Raspberries

What Is in the Fruits Group?

by Brian P. Cleary

illustrations by Martin Goneau

consultant Jennifer K. Nelson, Master of Science, Registered Dietitian, Licensed Dietitian

Ｍ Millbrook Press · Minneapolis

Some fruits are juicy,
while others are dried.

Some have a core
and some seeds deep inside.

Some fruits
are sweet,

while others
are sour.

And they help keep us healthy
with vitamin power!

So what is a fruit?
It's the usually sweet,
fleshy part of a plant
that we're able to eat.

An Apple
a day
keeps the
doctors
happy!

Fruit
Power

They often are tasty,
and most doctors say

we should eat several times
from this food group each day.

Many, like apples
and pears,
grow on trees.

We often use ladders
to pick fruit from these.

A grove or an orchard
is where you will find

a group of such trees
in a cluster or line.

Tangerines, oranges,

a grapefruit or cherry—
these are a few
of the fruits that trees carry.

10

While trees produce
plenty of peaches
and plums

they do not grow pineapples
prickling our thumbs!

Unlike a fish,
there is no need to hook them.

You don't have to boil them, fry them,
or cook them.

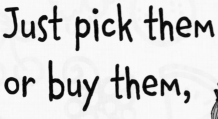

Just pick them
or buy them,

then wash them and
eat 'em.

Unlike lots of veggies,
you don't have to heat 'em!

The grape is a fruit
that is grown on a vine,

which makes a sweet juice
that is simply divine.

The kiwi,
another vine fruit,
is quite yummy.

Those fuzzy brown gems
are a treat for your tummy.

Bananas are cool
'cause they're packaged in peels.
They're equally good
on desserts or with meals.

16

A fruit when it's squeezed
will quite often produce

a fresh and delicious
and succulent juice.

Some, like orange, mango, and grapefruit, have pulp

and make you grow stronger with each sip or gulp.

19

For fruit high in fiber,
you may want to try a

raspberry,

blackberry,

even papaya!

A plum or a prune or some nice honeydew—

all these will help us
to go "number two."

A grape that's laid out
in the sun to be dried

turns into a raisin—less juicy inside.

And plums that are dried yield something that's neat:

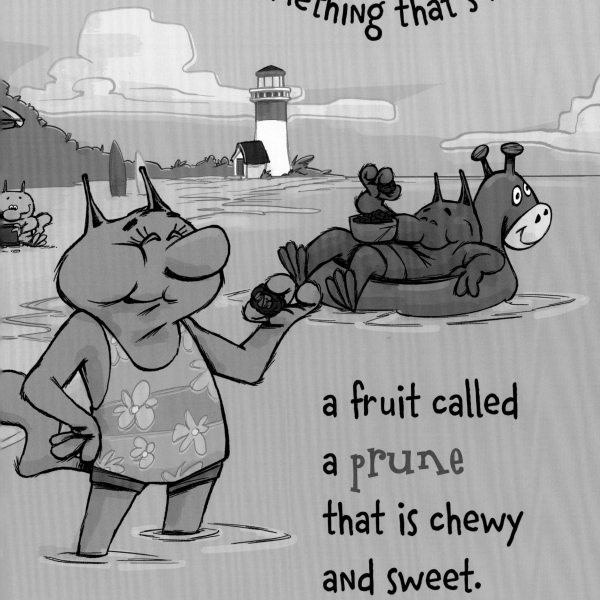

a fruit called a prune that is chewy and sweet.

Bakers use fruits
for desserts we can buy

like an apricot, pear,
or a blueberry pie.

Apples for dumplings
and strudels with cherries,
peaches for cobblers
and tarts filled with berries.

It keeps your gums healthy and strengthens them too.

So have some more fruit, and your mouth will thank you!

Next time
you're drinking
a smoothie
or shake

or peeling some fruit
for a salad you'll make,

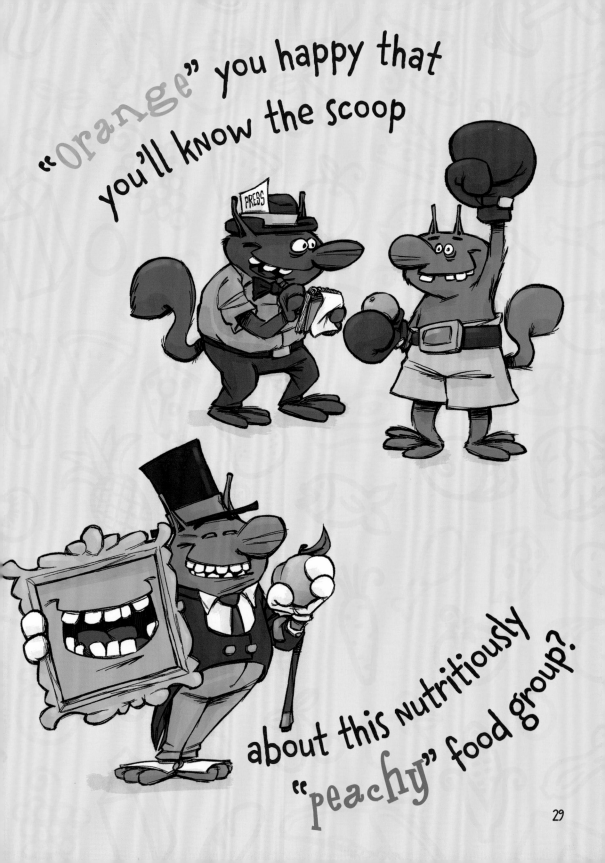

So what is in the fruits group? Do you know?

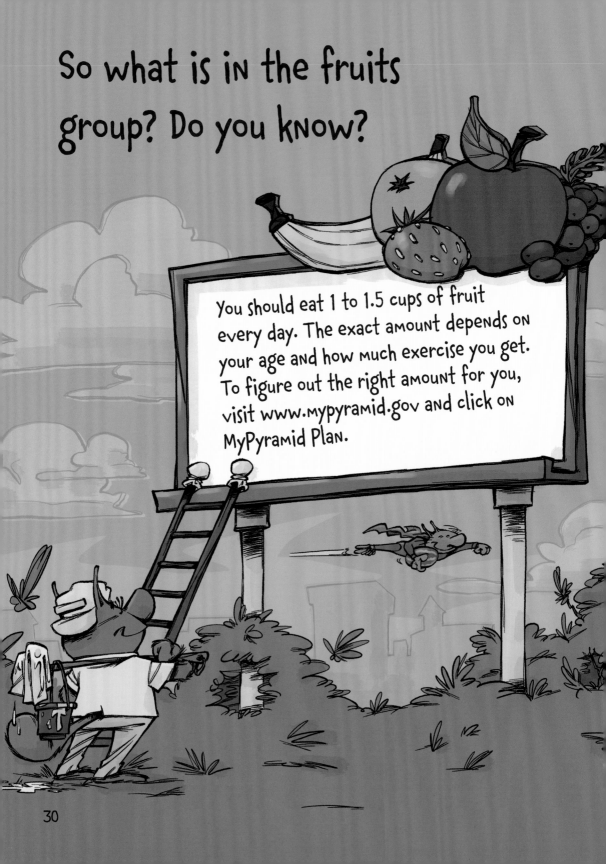

You should eat 1 to 1.5 cups of fruit every day. The exact amount depends on your age and how much exercise you get. To figure out the right amount for you, visit www.mypyramid.gov and click on MyPyramid Plan.

1 small apple equals 1 cup

1 large banana equals 1 cup

1 cup of 100% orange juice equals 1 cup

8 large strawberries equals 1 cup

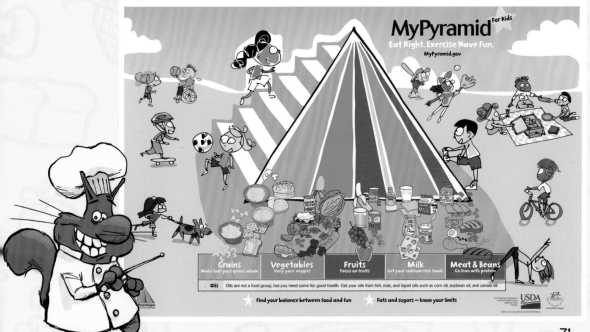

This book provides general
dietary information for children
ages 5–9 in accordance with the
MyPyramid guidelines created by the
United States Department of Agriculture (USDA).
The information in this book is not intended as medical advice. Anyone with food allergies
or sensitivities should follow the advice of a physician or other medical professional.

Find activities, games, and more at
www.brianpcleary.com

ABOUT THE AUTHOR, ILLUSTRATOR & CONSULTANT

BRIAN P. CLEARY is the author of the Words Are Categorical®, Math Is Categorical®,
Adventures in Memory™, Sounds Like Reading®, and Food Is CATegorical™ series,
as well as several picture books and poetry books. He lives in Cleveland, Ohio.

MARTIN GONEAU is the illustrator of the Food Is CATegorical™ series. He lives in
Trois-Rivières, Québec.

JENNIFER K. NELSON is Director of Clinical Dietetics and Associate Professor in
Nutrition at Mayo Clinic in Rochester, Minnesota. She is also a Specialty Medical
Editor for nutrition and healthy eating content for MayoClinic.com.

Text copyright © 2011 by Brian P. Cleary
Illustrations copyright © 2011 by Lerner Publishing Group, Inc.

Millbrook Press
A division of Lerner Publishing Group, Inc.
241 First Avenue North
Minneapolis, MN 55401 U.S.A.

Website address: www.lernerbooks.com

Library of Congress Cataloging-in-Publication Data

Cleary, Brian P., 1959-
    Apples, cherries, red raspberries : what is in the fruits group? / by Brian P. Cleary ; illustrated by Martin Goneau ;
consultant, Jennifer K. Nelson.
        p.   cm. — (Food Is CATegorical)
    ISBN: 978-1-58013-589-4 (lib. bdg. : alk. paper)
    1. Fruits—Juvenile literature. 2. Fruit in human nutrition—Juvenile literature. I. Goneau, Martin. II. Nelson, Jennifer K.
III. Title.
    TX397.C54 2010
    641.3'4—dc22   2009049582

Manufactured in the United States of America
1 – PC – 7/15/10